CLASSICS FOR THE DEVE[LOPING PIANIST]
CORE REPERTOIRE FOR STUDY AND PERFORMANCE
[S]elected and Edited by Ingrid Jacobson Clarfield and Phyllis Alpert Lehrer

This book is dedicated to our wonderful children and their fabulous spouses: Julie and Michael Gordon; Natasha and Jeffrey Lehrer; Suzanne Lehrer and Jonathan LeBouef; and Amanda and E. J. Newell.

Alfred Music
P.O. Box 10003
Van Nuys, CA 91410-0003
alfred.com

ISBN-10: 0-7390-7896-8
ISBN-13: 978-0-7390-7896-9

FOREWORD

The five books in this series present 100 pieces the editors believe developing pianists should study and perform. Each book contains 20 pieces selected from the four main style periods. The pieces in Book 3 are appropriate for late-intermediate pianists. The editors suggest learning pieces from different eras to appreciate, through comparison and contrast, the characteristics that define each style.

EDITORIAL SUGGESTIONS

The editors have provided primary and alternate fingers (in parentheses) to facilitate musicality and technique. Pianists should experiment with each fingering and use the one that is most comfortable for them. Once fingering preferences have been established, cross out the alternatives to avoid confusion.

The composers' indications for dynamics and articulation are provided as well as the editors' additional suggestions to help the pianist achieve greater musical expression, better balance, and create clear voicing. Indications such as *f* – *p* mean that the section is to be played *f* the first time and *p* on the repeat. Double dynamic markings are sometimes provided to aid with balance between voices. For example, the melody may be marked *mf* with an accompanying voice marked *pp*.

Ornaments should only be added after the piece has been learned solidly and when the student is comfortable technically.

Metronome markings are suggested within a wide range to allow pianists to find a tempo at which they can perform the music comfortably and artistically.

ADDITIONAL REPERTOIRE

The following listing includes additional late-intermediate repertoire from the 20th century. Copyright restrictions did not allow them to be included in this volume. The editors believe that pianists also will enjoy studying these well-loved pieces.

Ernst Bloch (1880-1959) . . . . *Pastorale* (from *Enfantines*)

Alfredo Casella (1883-1959). . . . . *Siciliana*, Op. 35, No. 6 (from *Eleven Children's Pieces*)

Alberto Ginastera (1916-1983). . . . . . . *American Prelude No. 6* (Tribute to
Roberto Garcia Morillo), Op. 12, No. 6
(from *Twelve American Preludes*)

Dmitri Kabalevsky (1904-1987). . . . . . *Sonatina in C Major*, Op. 13, No. 1

Aram Khatchaturian (1903-1978) . . . . *Sonatina*

Octavio Pinto (1890-1950). . . . . *Run, Run* (from *Scenas infantis*)

Sergei Prokofiev (1891-1953) . . . . *Tarantella*, Op. 65, No. 4 (from *Music for Children*)

Dmitri Shostakovich (1906-1975) . . . . *Fantastic Dance No. 2* (Andantino), Op. 5, No. 2
(from *Three Fantastic Dances*)

ACKNOWLEDGMENTS

With heartfelt appreciation to the people who helped us with this project:

Special thanks to Dean Elder and Kristen Topham who helped us immensely on all five books. We are forever grateful!

With gratitude to our colleagues at Alfred for their support and help on this project: Sharon Aaronson, Tom Gerou, E. L. Lancaster, Linda Lusk, Albert Mendoza, and Bruce Nelson.

Additional thanks to Lauren Exley, Debbie Williamson, and Richard Woo.

Gavotte

(from *French Suite No. 5 in G Major*)

Johann Sebastian Bach
(1685–1750)
BWV 816

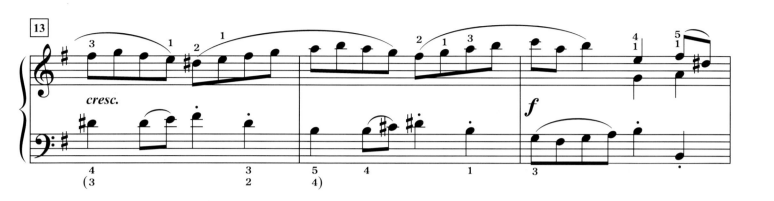

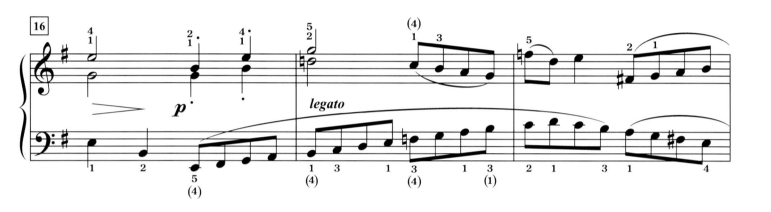

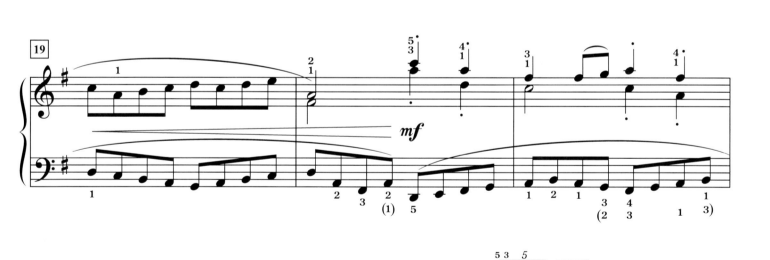

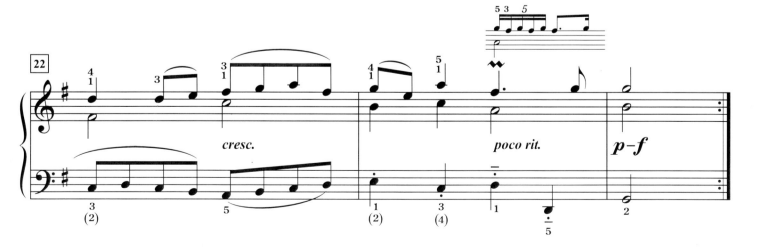

Invention No. 8 in F Major

Johann Sebastian Bach
(1685–1750)
BWV 779

* Play eighth notes detached in m. 1 and throughout, except where slurs are indicated.
All sixteenth notes are played with an articulated legato.

7

Invention No. 13 in A Minor

Johann Sebastian Bach
(1685–1750)
BWV 784

9

Prelude in C Major

(from *The Well-Tempered Clavier, Vol. I*)

Johann Sebastian Bach
(1685–1750)
BWV 846

Moderato (♩ = 72–88)

p *legato*

mp

p

f

simile

p

f

mp

mf

p

* Pedal optional every two beats.

11

Sonata in C Major

Domenico Scarlatti
(1685–1757)
K. 159; L. 104

* Scarlatti's trills begin on the main note.
** Scarlatti's appoggiaturas begin on the note above.

13

* Lower octave notes are optional.

15

Für Elise

Ludwig van Beethoven
(1770–1827)
WoO 59

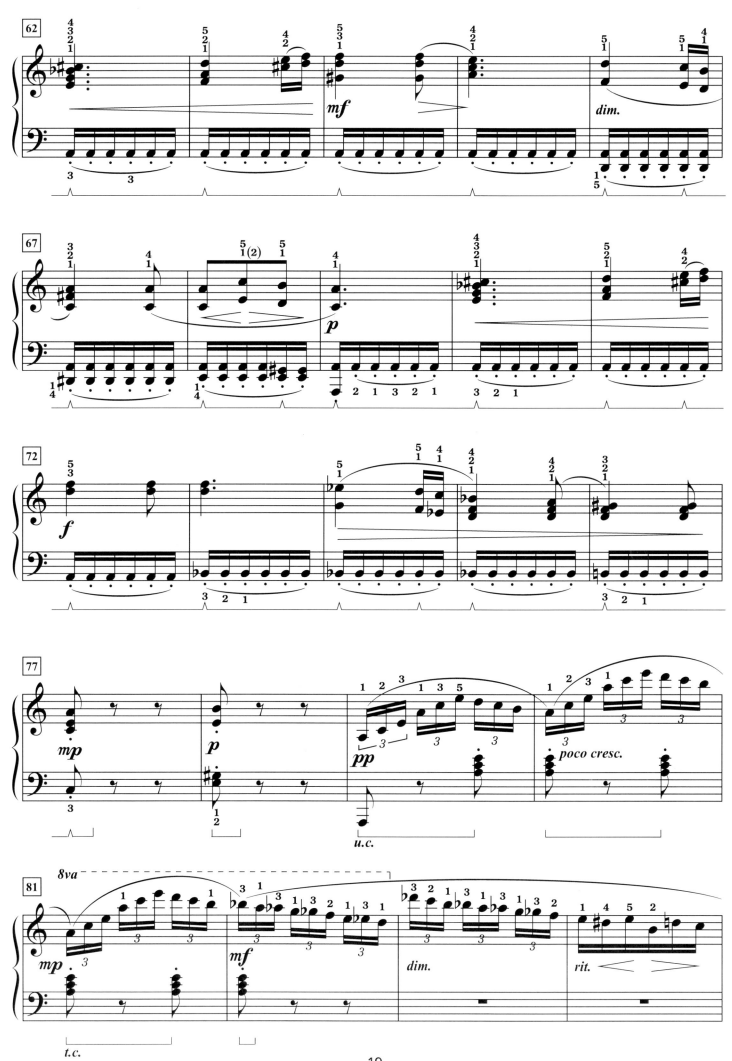

19

20

Bagatelle in G Minor

Ludwig van Beethoven
(1770-1827)
Op. 119, No. 1

Sonata in G Major

III

Franz Joseph Haydn
(1732–1809)
Hob. XVI/27

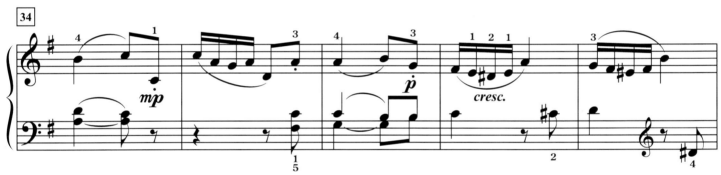

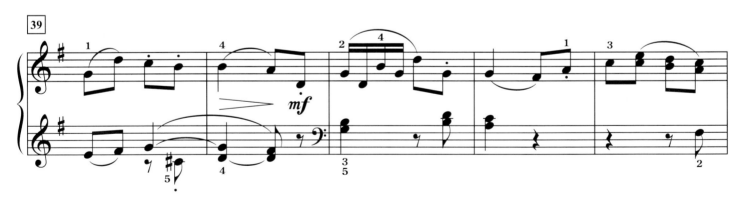

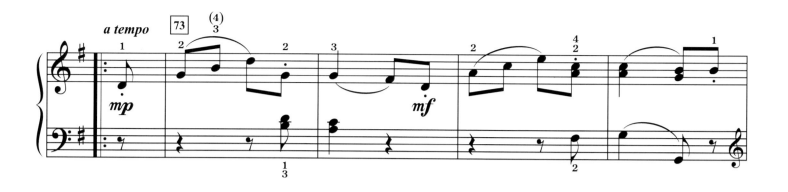

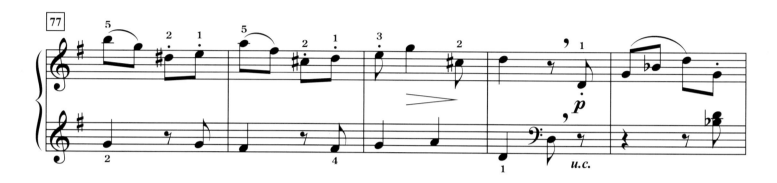

27

Sonatina in F Major

I

Anton Diabelli
(1781–1858)
Op. 151, No. 3

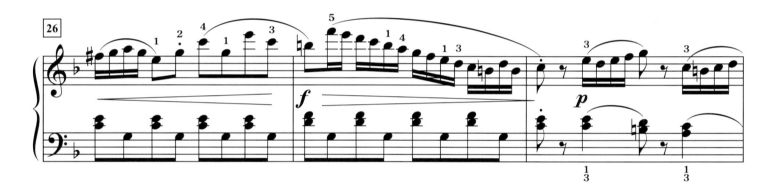

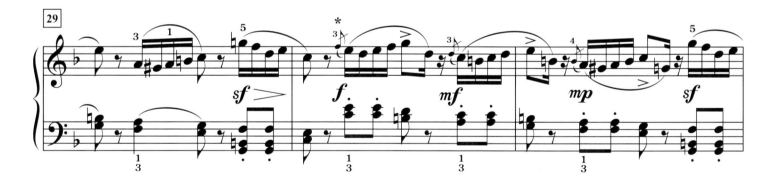

* Play the short appoggiatura very quickly, almost together with the main note.

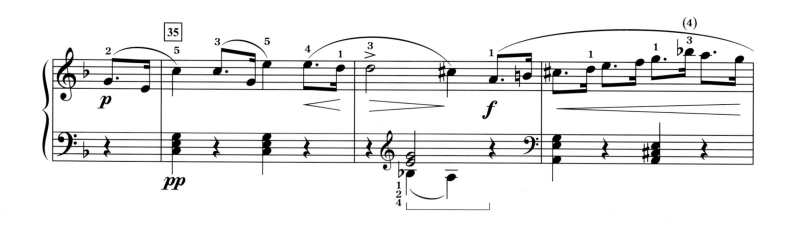

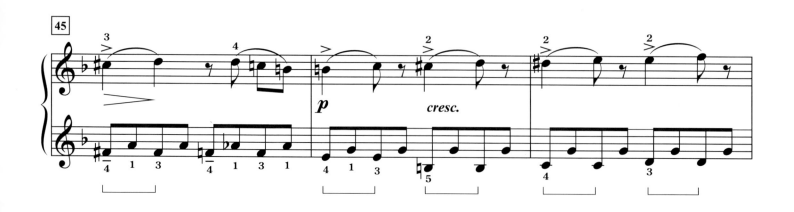

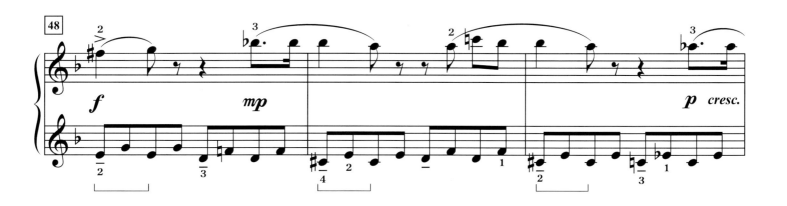

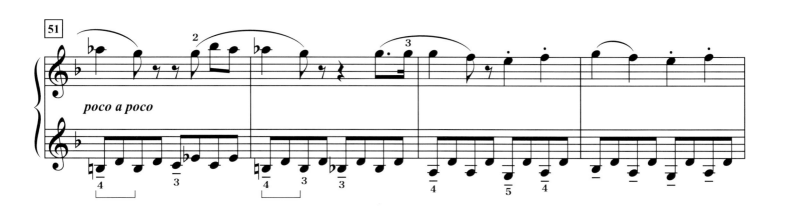

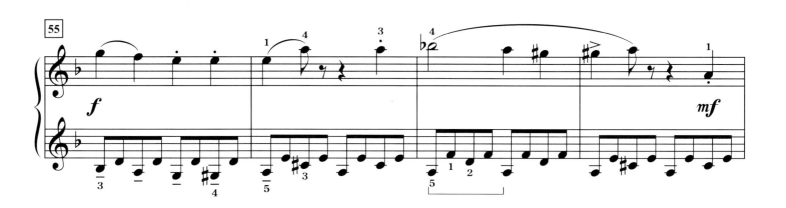

Sonata in C Major

I

Wolfgang Amadeus Mozart
(1756–1791)
K. 545

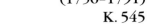

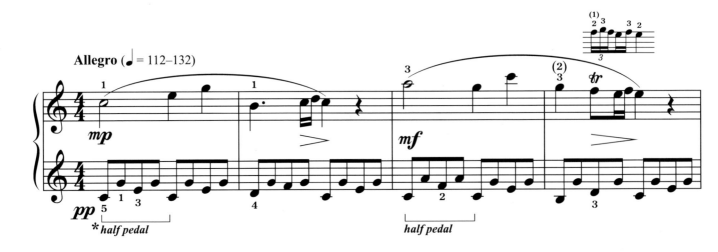

* Use half pedal, or hold the first eighth note of each four-note group (finger pedal).

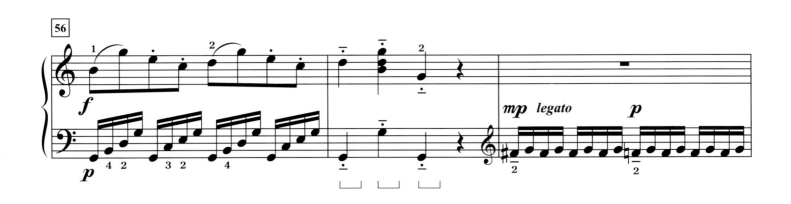

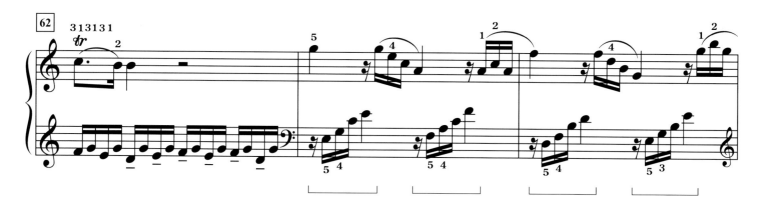

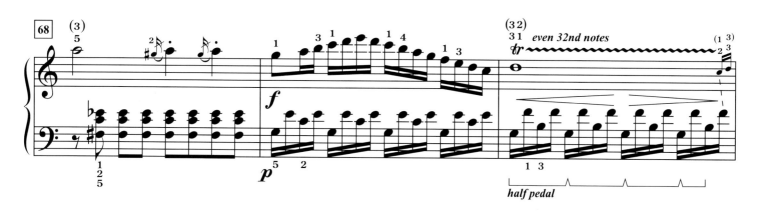

Mazurka in G Minor

Frédéric Chopin
(1810–1849)
Op. 67, No. 2, Posth.

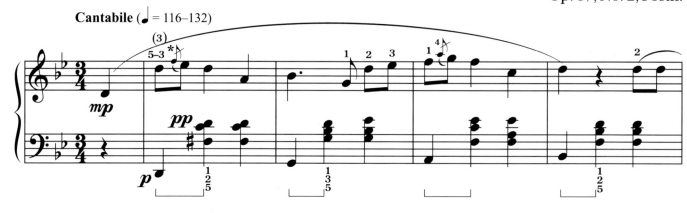

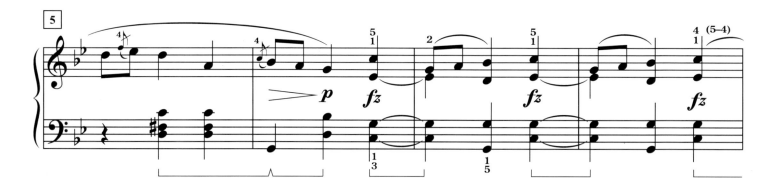

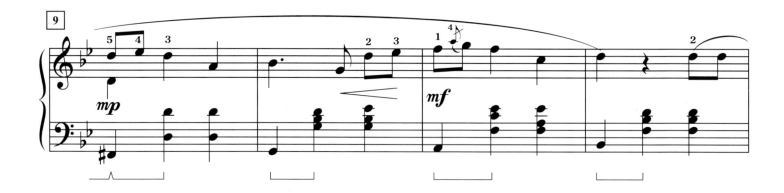

*Play grace notes on the beat.

42

44

Waltz in A Minor

Frédéric Chopin
(1810–1849)
Op. Posth.

* Many pianists play this A an octave lower.

47

Song without Words

("Consolation")

Felix Mendelssohn
(1809–1847)
Op. 30, No. 3

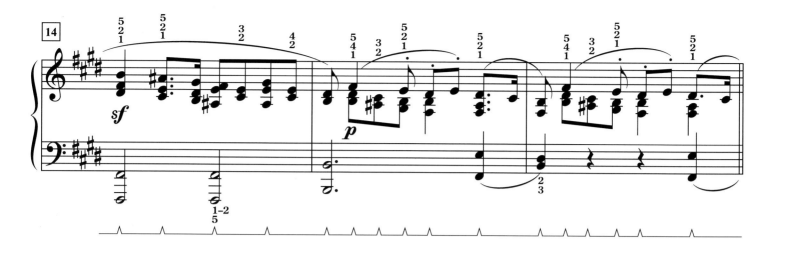

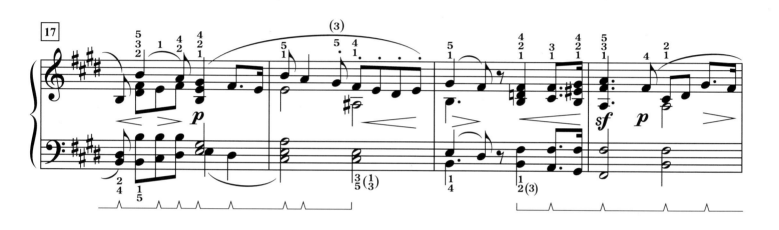

49

Knecht Ruprecht*

(from *Album for the Young*)

Robert Schumann
(1810–1856)
Op. 68, No. 12

---

* Knecht Ruprecht (Knight Rupert) is a German folk figure who is a helper of Saint Nicholas at Christmas time, giving sticks, stones, and other unwanted gifts to naughty children, and sweets to good children.

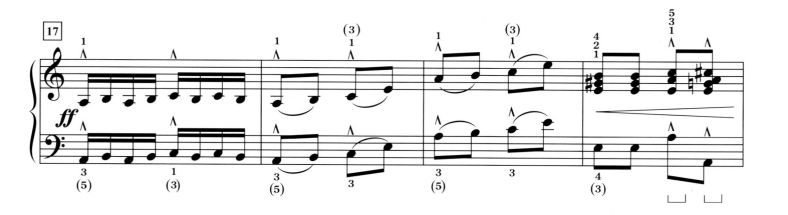

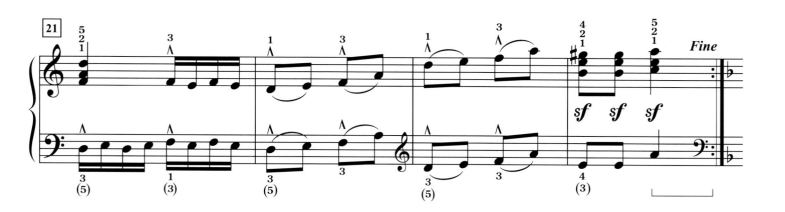

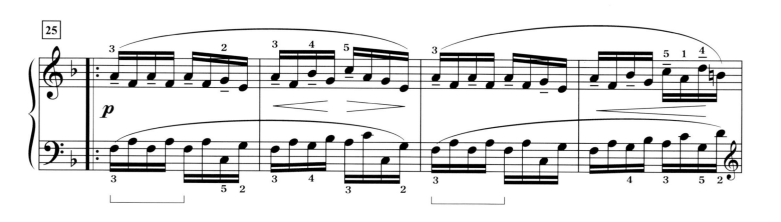

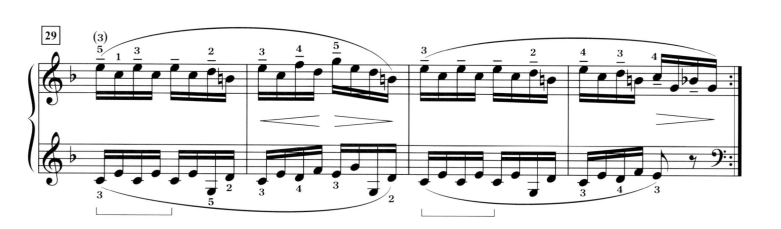

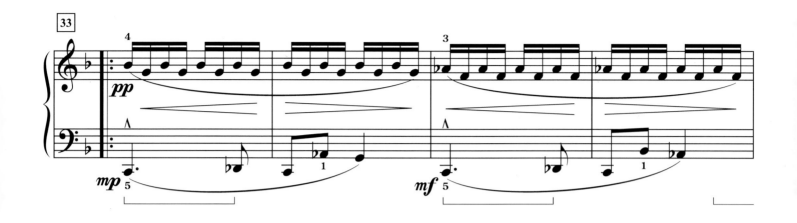

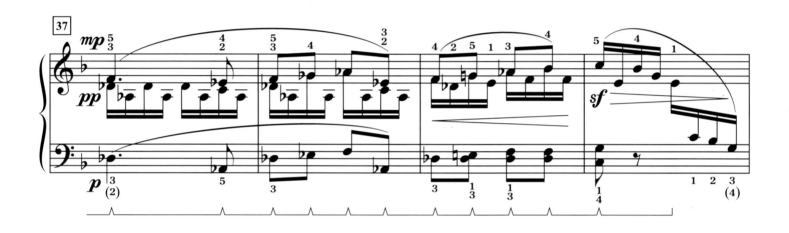

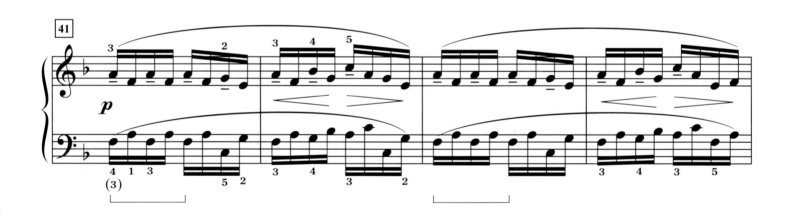

D. C. al Fine
(without repeat)

About Foreign Lands and People

(from *Scenes from Childhood*)

Robert Schumann
(1810-1856)
Op. 15, No. 1

Andante con moto (♩ = 76–92)

* The editors suggest to bring out the bass line in mm. 9–14 on the repeat.

Le petit nègre

Claude Debussy
(1862-1918)

* Play the grace note quickly before the beat.

57

Valse poético no. 3

Enrique Granados
(1867–1916)

* Roll quickly if you cannot reach.

Valse poético no. 4

Enrique Granados
(1867–1916)

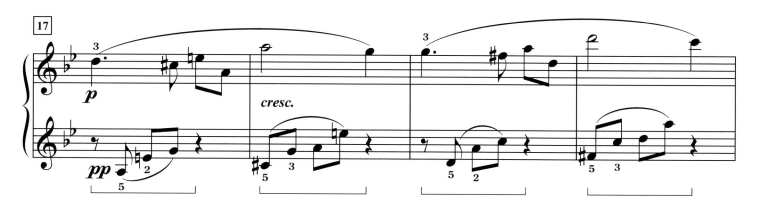

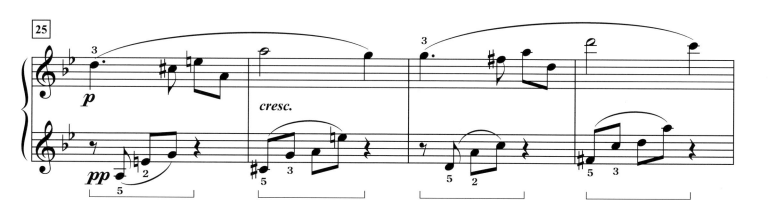

Bagatelle

Alexander Tcherepnin
(1899–1977)
Op. 5, No. 1

Allegro marziale (𝅗𝅥 = 88–100)

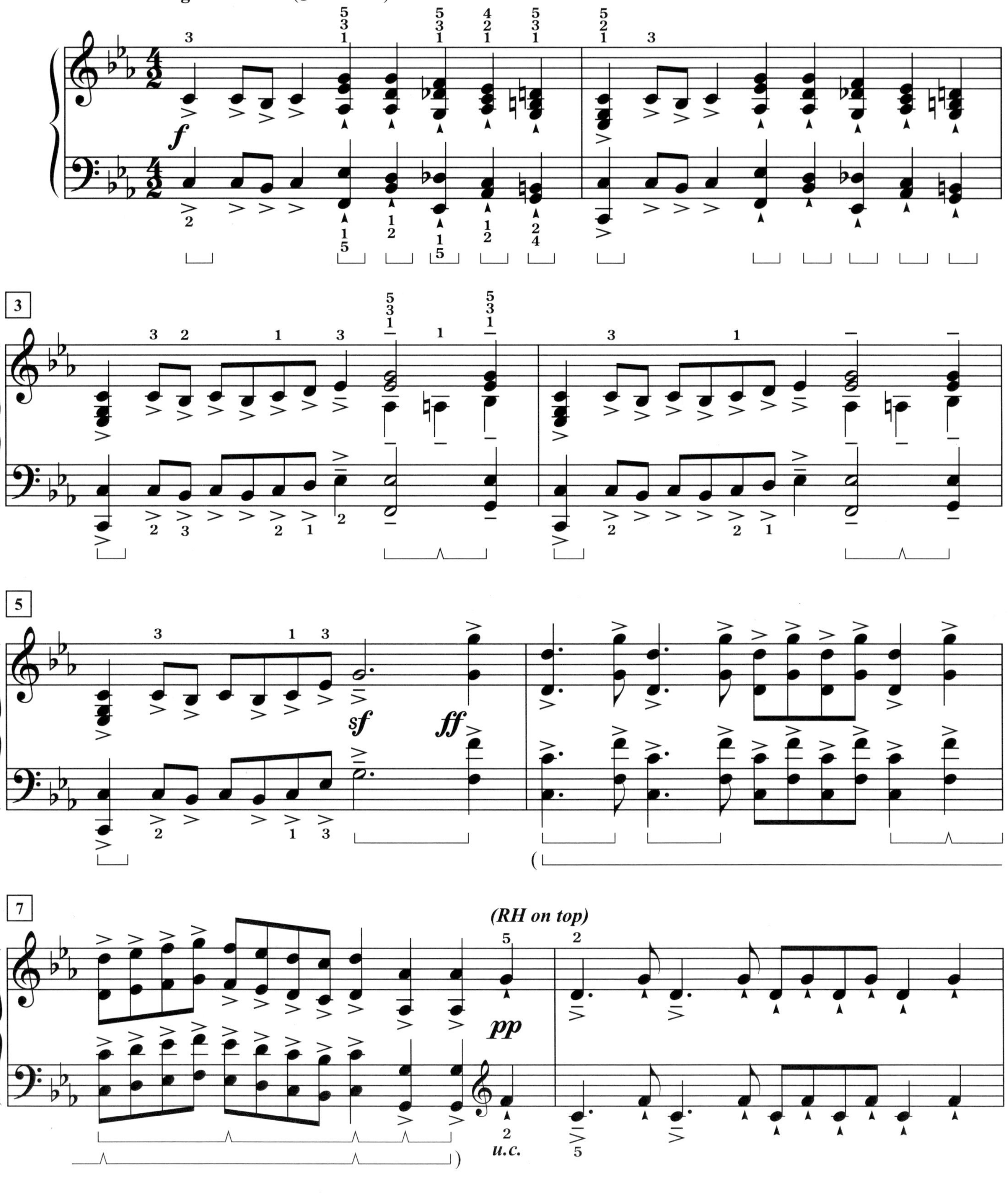

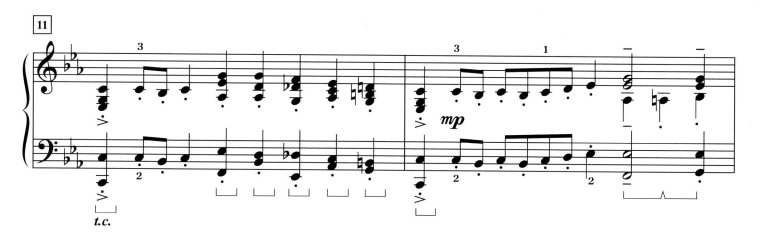

t.c.

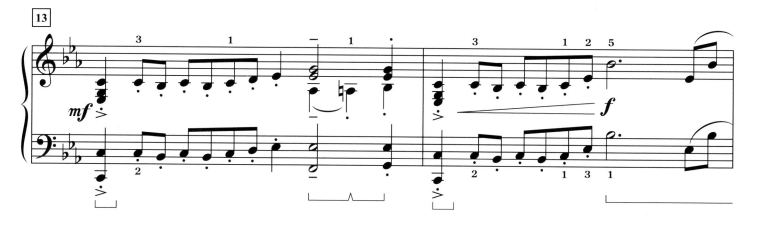

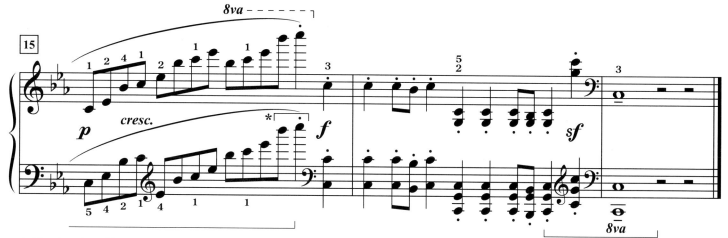

* May be played by RH to simplify leap.

63

Bagatelle

Alexander Tcherepnin
(1899–1977)
Op. 5, No. 10